I0165215

Danger in Seattle

I Talk You Talk Press

Copyright © 2018 I Talk You Talk Press

ISBN: 978-4-907056-80-3

www.italkyoutalk.com

info@italkyoutalk.com

All rights reserved. No part of this publication may be resold, reproduced, stored in retrieval system, copied in any form or by any means, electronic, mechanical, photocopying, recording or otherwise transmitted without the prior written permission from the publisher. You must not circulate this publication in any format, online or otherwise.

This is a work of fiction. Names, characters, businesses, organizations, products, places, events and incidents are either the products of the author's imagination or are used in a fictitious manner. We have no affiliation with any existing companies mentioned in this story. Any resemblance to actual persons, living or dead, existing stories or actual events is purely coincidental.

Although the author and publisher have made every effort to ensure that the contents of this book were correct at press time, the author and publisher do not assume and hereby disclaim any liability to any party for any loss, damage, or disruption caused by errors or omissions, whether such errors or omissions result from negligence, accident, or any other cause.

For more information, see the Copyright Notice on our website.

Image copyright: © Benjamin Haas - Fotolia.com #17668766 Standard License
© loslena - Fotolia.com #71364176 Standard License

CONTENTS

Chapter One   1

Chapter Two   3

Chapter Three   7

Chapter Four   9

Chapter Five   12

Chapter Six   15

Chapter Seven   18

Chapter Eight   21

Thank You   26

About the Author   28

CHAPTER ONE

Giovanna was happy. She was on an aeroplane. She was flying from New York to Seattle to visit Isabel. It was Giovanna's first time to visit Seattle.

Isabel was an old friend from high school in New York. She worked in an office in Seattle. When they were high school students, they played tennis together. They were members of the school tennis team.

Ten years later, they met again on Facebook. They messaged each other. They told each other about their lives. After high school, Giovanna went to university in Los Angeles and Isabel went to university in Texas. Then, Giovanna went home to New York and got a job in an office. Isabel got a job in an office in Seattle. Isabel still played tennis every weekend. She was a member of a tennis club. Giovanna told Isabel about her daily life in New York. Living in New York was very expensive and Giovanna did not earn very much money.

--- *'I want to travel.'*--- Giovanna messaged Isabel. --- *'I am saving hard.'*---

Then something wonderful happened. Giovanna won first prize in a lottery.

She sent a message to Isabel.

--- *'I won $2 million dollars! I will stop working. I can travel anywhere! Someday, I will buy a house, but just now, I have put all the money in the bank. It is a wonderful feeling to have so much money. I look at my bank account all the time!'*---

--- *'Before you travel overseas and buy a house, why don't you visit me here?'*---

1

messaged Isabel. ---'*Come soon. We can celebrate your good news together!*'---

Giovanna thought it was a good idea. Only three weeks after she won the money, she was travelling to Seattle. She planned to stay with Isabel for eight days.

Giovanna took her phone out of her bag and looked at the last email from Isabel.

---'*Hi Giovanna! I'm looking forward to seeing you. We will have a great time. I haven't seen you for ten years, but I have your photograph. I'm sure I will know you when I see you at the airport. When we were at school, people always said to us, 'You look like sisters!' See you soon!*' ---

I'm looking forward to seeing her, thought Giovanna. *At school, we were not very close friends, but I liked her. I enjoyed playing tennis with her.*

Giovanna fell asleep. When she woke up, the plane was landing. She looked out of the window. It was late afternoon and the autumn sky was cloudy. She got off the plane, picked up her suitcase, and went out into the arrivals hall. She looked around.

Where is Isabel? she thought. *She is not here.*

CHAPTER TWO

Just then, a man walked towards her. He was looking at a photograph on his smartphone. He looked at the photograph and he looked at Giovanna.

"Excuse me, are you Giovanna?" he asked.

"Yes, I am," she said.

"I'm Stuart. I'm Isabel's friend. She can't come to the airport. She has to work. So she asked me to come here to meet you."

"Oh," said Giovanna. "But she is on vacation this week."

"Yes, but it was an emergency. She had to go to the office. Come on, give me your suitcase. I will take you to her apartment now."

"OK, that's very kind of you. Thank you."

Stuart picked up Giovanna's suitcase, and she followed him to the car park.

"It's that blue Toyota," said Stuart, pointing to a car.

"How long will it take to get to her apartment?" asked Giovanna.

"Oh, about thirty minutes," said Stuart.

"How do you know Isabel?" asked Giovanna. "Do you work together?"

"We met at a party," he said.

"Oh, I see," said Giovanna.

Stuart put her suitcase in the back of the car. Then, they got in the car, and drove out of the car park.

Isabel lives in the city, thought Giovanna. *I saw her apartment on Google Earth. She lives near the Space Needle. It's very convenient.*

Giovanna enjoyed looking out of the car window. After about 20 minutes, she could see the Space Needle.

That's strange, she thought. *We aren't going in the direction of the Space Needle.*

"Isabel lives near the Space Needle. Is this a different road to the Space Needle?" she asked.

"Yes, the other road is very busy. It's rush hour now," said Stuart. "This is the quickest way."

"OK," said Giovanna. She was feeling tired and hungry.

Giovanna took a bottle of water and some cookies out of her bag.

"Do you want a cookie?" asked Giovanna.

"No thanks," said Stuart.

We have been driving for a long time, she thought. She looked at the time on her phone. *Forty-five minutes. Well, it is rush hour, so I'm sure it will take longer.*

She looked at the road sign. *University area,* she thought. *The university is north of the Space Needle. Why are we going this way? This is strange.*

"I'm going to call Isabel," she said.

"Don't do that," said Stuart.

"Pardon? Why not?" asked Giovanna.

"She is at work." Stuart looked a little worried.

This is strange, thought Giovanna. *Why doesn't he want me to call her?*

"I'll call her cell phone," she said.

She called Isabel, but Isabel didn't answer.

"I told you," said Stuart. "She is at work."

"I'm sorry," said Giovanna.

She looked at him. *This isn't right,* she thought. *It doesn't feel right.*

She had a bad feeling about Stuart. He seemed angry.

Then, the car stopped at a red traffic light.

Without thinking, Giovanna undid her seatbelt and jumped out of the car. She started to run.

"Hey! Come back! Hey!" shouted Stuart.

But Giovanna did not go back. She ran for about five minutes. Then she stopped. She looked around. She was near the university buildings. There were many students walking around. She saw a bench and sat down.

Why did I run? Who is Stuart? Why do I feel like I am in danger? Stuart has my suitcase! Why did I do that?

She tried to call Isabel again. There was no answer.

She thought for a few minutes. It was starting to get cold.

Should I go to Isabel's apartment? Or is it dangerous? Or am I crazy? Maybe I should stay in a hotel tonight. But I should go to the apartment. Isabel might be in trouble. She might need my help. But…

She stood up and walked to the main road. She stopped a taxi.

"Where do you want to go?" asked the taxi driver.

"To the Space Needle please," she said.

She looked at the time. It was seven o'clock. The taxi drove through the city.

My suitcase is in Stuart's car, she thought. *All my clothes are in it! It's lucky I have money. If I can't get my suitcase back, I will go shopping tomorrow.*

She looked out of the taxi window at the city lights. She could see the Space Needle getting closer.

After around 20 minutes, the taxi stopped near the Space Needle. She paid the driver and got out of the taxi. It was a cold evening, but there were still many people around. She followed the map on her phone to Isabel's apartment building.

There it is! she thought. *It's that tall building, and she lives on the third floor.*

She looked up at the third floor. The third floor was dark.

She isn't home, she thought. *She must still be at work.* Then she saw a man standing near the entrance to the building.

That's Stuart! she thought. *I don't want him to see me.*

She took her hat out of her pocket and put it on. Then, she walked quickly down a dark side street and stopped.

He didn't see me. But what am I going to do? she thought. *He is waiting for someone. Maybe he is waiting for me. So where is Isabel? Should I call her?*

She tried to call Isabel again. There was no answer. She looked around and saw a blue Toyota parked on the street.

That's Stuart's car! she thought. *I'm sure there is a problem with Isabel. I'm sure Stuart knows something about it. How can I find her? Is Stuart waiting for me? If he is waiting for me, he won't wait forever. He will go. I have to follow his car. But how can I follow it? By taxi? No…*

Then, she had an idea. *Maybe I could rent a car. But will any car rental offices still be open?*

She looked at her phone. It was 8:00pm. She searched for rental car companies in the city.

There are a few places near here, she thought. *I can call them.*

She called one of the places. A woman answered.

"Hi, I need to rent a car tonight," said Giovanna.

"Do you have a reservation?" asked the woman.

"No, I don't, but it's really urgent. Can I pick a car up in about ten minutes?"

"I'm sorry. We are closed. The earliest you can rent a car is tomorrow morning, we can't...."

"It's urgent. I really need a car!" said Giovanna.

"Where are you?" asked the woman.

"I'm near the Space Needle."

"There is a small rental car place near there. Why don't you try them?"

The woman gave her the address and phone number of the other company.

Giovanna put the address into Google Maps and hurried to the office. It was still open.

She walked into the office. A man was sitting behind a desk.

"Please help me," she said. "It's urgent. I need to rent a car tonight."

The man said, "You are lucky. We are usually closed at this time, but I am working late. I can rent you a car."

CHAPTER THREE

Twenty minutes later, Giovanna was driving through the streets to Isabel's apartment. It started to rain heavily.

I hope Stuart's car is still here, she thought. She drove down the small side street near Isabel's apartment, and saw the blue Toyota.

Stuart is still here! Good! she thought.

She parked a few metres behind the car and waited. After a few minutes, Stuart came round the corner and walked to the car. Giovanna watched him. He didn't see her because it was dark.

Stuart got in the Toyota and drove away. Giovanna waited for a few seconds, and then followed his car through the rainy streets. She didn't want to drive too close to his car. Luckily, another car came in front of her.

Good, she thought. *He won't see me.*

Giovanna looked at the road signs.

We are going north, she thought. *We are going up towards the university. I remember this road. Stuart and I drove along this road.*

They drove farther north, past the university.

Where are we going? she thought.

Giovanna couldn't see very well because it was dark and raining, but the houses looked big and expensive.

The small streets were quiet. A few cars were parked at the sides of the road.

This is dangerous, she thought. *If I am not careful, he will see my car. There are not many cars driving on these roads.*

She looked in her car mirror. There was a car behind her. She stopped at the side of the road and waited for a few seconds. The car behind passed her, and then she started to follow Stuart's car again. After a while, Stuart's car stopped outside a house. Giovanna continued down the road, then she turned a corner and stopped. It was a quiet street and the houses were large. She looked at the map on her smartphone.

This area is called Roosevelt, she thought. She waited for a few minutes and then got out of the car and walked to the other street.

She walked quickly to Stuart's car. Giovanna couldn't see the house because there were many tall trees in the front garden.

The garden is very big. The owner must be rich, she thought. She looked around. No one was there.

She walked through the gate and into the garden. She could see the house. The lights were on. She walked very quietly to the back of the house. The curtains were closed so she couldn't see anything, but she could hear voices. Two men and a woman.

Is that Isabel's voice? She tried to listen carefully. *I don't know,* she thought. *I haven't spoken to her for ten years.*

She sat below a window. She could hear a man talking, but it was raining heavily, so she couldn't hear his words clearly.

What should I do? Should I call the police? But what can I tell the police? Stuart hasn't done anything bad to me. And what can I tell the police about Isabel? Maybe she is working. Maybe this is Stuart's house, and the woman in there is his wife. Maybe I'm thinking too much…The police will think I am crazy!

She walked back to her car. Her clothes and hair were very wet.

I want to change clothes, and I need a towel, but I don't have my suitcase! she thought.

She drove back around the corner and parked about twenty metres from Stuart's car. She tried to call Isabel again, but there was no answer.

I'll stay here, she thought. *I'll stay in the car and watch the house. I'm hungry and wet, but I can wait until morning.*

Giovanna thought about her day.

This is a bad start to my trip! I hope it gets better tomorrow. I hope I can find Isabel. Very soon, Giovanna fell asleep.

CHAPTER FOUR

Giovanna woke up and looked at the time. It was 5:00am, and it was still dark.

I slept for many hours, but Stuart's car is still there. That's lucky, she thought. *I was very tired. Now I need coffee.*

She got out of the car and walked to the gate of the house. She looked at the house through the trees. It was still dark.

I will try to find a convenience store and buy some coffee and breakfast.

She checked the map on her phone. There was a convenience store about a ten-minute drive away.

She found the convenience store and bought some coffee, a muffin, yoghurt and chocolate. She went to the bathroom and looked in the mirror.

I look tired, she thought. *But I can't rest until I find Isabel.*

She went to the car and drove back to the house. This time, she parked on the other side of the street. She thought about Isabel while she was eating breakfast.

I hope she is OK, she thought. *Why hasn't she phoned me? Why hasn't she sent me a message?*

After about an hour, she saw more cars on the street. The drivers were businessmen and women, going to work. Giovanna put her phone next to her ear. People looked at her, but they thought she was a driver taking a telephone call.

Much later, she saw Stuart come out of the house and get into his car. He was alone. She put her head down so he couldn't see her. She heard his car drive away. She waited a few minutes. Then, she got out of the car and walked into the garden. She walked quietly around to the back of the house.

Is the back door open? she thought. She pushed the door, but it was locked.

What should I do? Should I try to get into the house? Should I knock on the door?

She looked through the window. It was a kitchen. A woman was making coffee. The woman was Isabel!

"Isabel!" shouted Giovanna. She knocked on the window.

Isabel looked very surprised. She ran to the window and opened it a little.

"What are you doing here? How did you find me?" she said quietly.

"But Isabel," said Giovanna. "Why are you here? Are you OK?"

Isabel didn't say anything for a few seconds. Then, she said, "Go away! It's dangerous."

"Dangerous?" asked Giovanna.

"Yes," said Isabel. "Dangerous for me, and dangerous for you. They will kill me if they know you are here. Go away!"

"What? Who are they? What are you talking about?" asked Giovanna.

"Shh!" said Isabel. "They will hear you!"

"Come on! Get out!" said Giovanna.

"No! Shh!" said Isabel. She shook her head. "I can't! The door is locked! They will see me! It's dangerous!"

"Who will see you?" asked Giovanna.

"Stuart has gone out, but there are two more men in the house," said Isabel.

Giovanna looked at her. *She looks very frightened,* she thought. *I have to help her. We have to go to the police.*

"Isabel, stay away from the door," she said.

"No Giovanna! It's too dangerous!"

Smash!!!

Giovanna kicked the back door and the lock broke. She pushed the door hard and it opened.

"Come on! Run!" shouted Giovanna.

"No!" said Isabel.

"What's wrong with you?" asked Giovanna. She ran into the kitchen and pulled Isabel out of the house.

"Hey! Stop!" A man came running from another room into the kitchen.

"Come on!" Giovanna took Isabel's hand, and Isabel and Giovanna ran through the garden to the car.

"Get in the car!" shouted Giovanna.

They jumped in the car and drove away. The man ran after the car, but then he stopped, took out his mobile phone and made a phone call.

CHAPTER FIVE

Giovanna drove very quickly through the streets. Soon she came to a main road. It was morning rush hour, so there were many cars. The cars were moving slowly.

"Where should we go?" she asked.

"I don't know this area very well. Give me your phone, I'll look at the map," said Isabel.

"What happened? Who is Stuart? Who are the other men? I was so worried about you! We have to go to the police!" said Giovanna.

"No, we can't do that," said Isabel. She was looking at the smartphone and typing something. "I'll tell you about it when we stop."

After a few minutes, Isabel pointed to the right and said, "Go this way. There is a big shopping mall with a large parking lot. No one will find us there."

She gave Giovanna directions to the mall.

After 15 minutes, they drove into the shopping mall car park. Giovanna stopped the car and looked at Isabel.

"Are you OK?" asked Giovanna.

"Yes, I am, but I am so sorry. This has been a bad start to your holiday," said Isabel.

They hugged each other. "It's great to see you! It's been such a long time!" said Giovanna.

Isabel smiled. "It's great to see you too."

"So, tell me everything," said Giovanna.

Isabel waited for a few seconds, and then she started to speak.

"A few weeks ago, I met a man at a party. We started talking. He seemed nice. We became friends on Facebook. One evening, he invited me for coffee. I said OK. So we had a kind of date. That night, I got your message. I read it on my smartphone. The message was about you winning the money.

"Then I went to the bathroom, I didn't take my phone. My phone was on the table. I think he looked at my phone, because after that, he asked many questions about you."

"Who is he?" asked Giovanna.

"Stuart. But I don't think Stuart is his real name. We went out a few times, but he always wanted to talk about you. So, yesterday, I was leaving my apartment, and two men were outside. One had a knife. He said, 'Get in the car'. I was frightened. So, I got in the car. Then, he took my phone and looked at your messages. They took me to that house in Roosevelt. Stuart came to the house last night. The two men are his friends. They said, 'We will kill your friend from New York if you try to escape.' So, I couldn't escape."

"Why did they do that?" asked Giovanna.

"They want your money," said Isabel.

"This is terrible! We should go to the police," said Giovanna.

"No! It's too dangerous," said Isabel.

"What? Why? But…"

Just then, Giovanna looked in the car mirror.

"I don't believe this! It's the car! It's Stuart! And there is another man with him! They followed us! How did they follow us? We have to go!" she shouted. Giovanna started the engine and drove out of the car park very quickly.

There were many cars on the road, so they couldn't go very fast. They were driving towards the city centre. They stopped at a red traffic light.

"They are behind us!" shouted Giovanna.

The lights changed. "I'll go this way," she said. "Maybe we can lose them in the backstreets."

They drove quickly through the backstreets. Stuart's car followed. Luckily, a truck came out of another street behind them, so Stuart could not see their car.

Giovanna turned a corner, and then another corner. She looked in the mirror.

"We've lost them!" she said. "I think we've lost them."

But she didn't stop. She drove south until they were near the airport.

CHAPTER SIX

Giovanna drove into a convenience store car park and stopped the car.

"I can't believe it! How did they find us? I don't understand!" she said.

Isabel didn't say anything.

"We have to call the police. Do you have my phone?" she said to Isabel.

"Yes, but maybe I should call them. Could you buy me a cup of coffee?" said Isabel.

"OK," said Giovanna. "I'll buy some food too."

She went into the convenience store. A few minutes later, she came out and got into the car.

"I got us some muffins and coffee," said Giovanna.

"I called the police," said Isabel. "The police will be here in a few minutes."

She gave the phone back to Giovanna. "Thank you for the coffee. Before I drink it, I must go to the restroom."

Giovanna sat in the car eating and drinking.

Five minutes later, she thought, *Isabel is taking a long time.*

A white car came into the car park and parked next to her. Two men wearing suits got out of the car.

One of them knocked on the window.

"We are detectives," he said. "I'm John Smith and this is my partner David Jones."

Giovanna smiled and got out of the car. "I'm Giovanna. My

friend Isabel called you. She is in the convenience store. I'm so glad you are here."

"We are going to take you to the police station. We can talk there," said John.

"OK, I'll tell Isabel," said Giovanna.

She went into the convenience store.

Where is Isabel? she thought. She walked around the store, but she could not see Isabel. She went to the restroom. The door was unlocked. She knocked on the door and then opened it. It was empty. Then, she saw the emergency exit door. It was open. She ran through the shop to the counter.

She said to the man behind the counter, "Excuse me, did you see the girl with black hair and a blue sweater? She came in here a few minutes ago."

"She went into the restroom," said the man.

"But she isn't there now! And the emergency exit door is open!" said Giovanna.

"What?" said the man.

Giovanna ran out of the store to the detectives.

"Isabel has gone!" she said.

"Get in the car," said John. "We have to find her!"

Giovanna got into the back of the car. She felt safe.

I've never been in a police car before, she thought.

She looked at her phone. *What's that? New app update?* She clicked on the link.

---Tracking app update---

What? What is this update? I haven't downloaded a tracking app. Did Isabel? But why?

Giovanna opened the app. It was tracking her location. She looked around the car.

This doesn't seem like a police car. There is no radio system or navigation. It just seems like a normal car, she thought.

"This car doesn't seem like a police car," she said. David turned around and smiled. "We are detectives," he said. "This isn't a patrol car."

Giovanna smiled. "Oh, I see."

The car was driving very fast along the road.

"Where are we going?" asked Giovanna.

"We are going to the police station," said John.

"But we have to find Isabel," said Giovanna.

"The patrol cars will look for her," said John.

But they haven't contacted the station. They haven't told anyone, thought Giovanna. *This is strange.*

Giovanna had a bad feeling about it. She looked at John. He had short brown hair. He was tall and around thirty years old. Then, she saw his key ring. It had a logo and the letters "NST" on it.

NST, she thought. *I've seen that before. That means North Seattle Tennis Club. Yes, that's the name of Isabel's tennis club. She put a picture up on Facebook a few weeks ago. These men are not police officers. They know Isabel! They are from her tennis club!*

David turned around. He saw her looking at the key ring.

"You are not policemen," she said.

John started to drive faster. David took out a gun.

"Shut up," he said. "Give me your phone."

Giovanna gave him her phone.

"And don't try to escape. If you try, we will kill you," he said.

CHAPTER SEVEN

They drove back north, towards the city.

Where are we going? Where are they taking me? thought Giovanna. *This is terrible!*

"Where are you taking me?" asked Giovanna.

"Shut up!" said John.

Giovanna looked around.

They are taking me to the house in Roosevelt, she thought.

Finally, they arrived at the house. John drove through the gates and parked the car at the back of the house. "Get out," he said.

She got out of the car. They walked into the house through the broken back door.

David pushed her into the living room.

"What are you going to do to me? What do you want?" asked Giovanna.

"We want your bank card, PIN number, ID cards and purse," said John. "Just give me your bag."

"I'm not giving you anything," said Giovanna.

David pointed his gun at her and said, "You will give us your bag and you will tell us your bank card PIN number."

"But, you can't use my bank card," said Giovanna. "There will be cameras in the bank."

"Don't worry about that," said John.

"Give me your bag! Now!" said David. "Don't make me angry!"

Giovanna gave him her bag. He opened it and took out her wallet. He opened the wallet and took out a card.

"Is this your bank card?" he asked.

"Yes."

"She has a driving license and credit cards," said David. "This will be enough."

He looked at Giovanna. "What's your PIN number?"

"And don't lie," said John. "David will stay with you until I come back. If you tell us the right number, we may let you live. If you tell us the wrong number, you will die."

"It's three zero one zero," said Giovanna.

David gave Giovanna's bag to John, and John walked out of the house. David stayed with Giovanna.

She heard John drive away. She looked at David.

"Why are you doing this? Who are you?" asked Giovanna. "Where is Isabel?"

"Shut up. Sit on that chair and shut up!" said David.

Giovanna sat down. David sat down too and watched her.

Giovanna looked around the living room. There was a very large TV, and there were big oil paintings on the walls. The armchair was very soft and comfortable.

This is a beautiful house, she thought. *Everything looks very expensive. But whose house is it?*

About two hours later, she heard a car.

John came into the house and smiled. "We got the money."

"What? How?" asked Giovanna. "You can't take my money!"

John did not answer her.

"What are we going to do with her?" asked David.

"Let's leave her here," said John. "Come on."

"You can't leave me here! And you can't take my money! You can't take my things!" shouted Giovanna.

"Goodbye!" said John. They walked out of the house and got in the car. Giovanna watched the car drive away.

What am I going to do? I have to call to the police, thought Giovanna. *But I don't have my phone. Maybe there is a phone in the house.*

She walked into the kitchen and saw a phone. She picked it up. There was no sound. *The phone is not working. I have to find someone to help me.*

She went out of the house and started to walk. It was a sunny afternoon. The street was very quiet. The houses looked empty.

Everyone is at work, she thought. *Which way should I go? Left or right? I'll go left. Maybe a car will come and I can get help.*

She walked for about ten minutes, and then she came to a bigger road.

She stood in the middle of the road and waved. The car slowed down. The driver was an old woman.

"Are you OK?" asked the old woman.

"Help me please! Call the police!" The woman parked the car at the side of the road.

"Get in the car," she said. "My name is Elsa." She took her phone out of her pocket and called the police.

CHAPTER EIGHT

Giovanna was in the police station. Elsa was sitting next to her. She told the policeman her story.

"We will look for the men," said the policeman. "Can you remember the address of the big house where you found Isabel?"

Giovanna shook her head. "No, I can't remember the address, but it was in an area called Roosevelt."

Then she remembered. "My phone! Isabel downloaded a tracking app on it! Maybe the men don't know! Or maybe they forgot! Maybe you can track it!"

"What's your phone number?" said the policeman.

Giovanna wrote it on a piece of paper and the policeman took it into another room. Another policeman brought coffee for Giovanna and Elsa. They drank the coffee while they waited.

"It is very kind of you to stay with me. But it's OK," Giovanna said to Elsa. "If you want to go, I will be fine."

Elsa took Giovanna's hand. "I want to stay with you. This is your first visit to Seattle and you are having a bad time. But Seattle is a very nice and friendly place. I want you to know that. So I want to help you."

The policeman came back about thirty minutes later and smiled.

"We found them!" he said. "We got the tracking information. They were in a different car, but they still had your phone. They were on their way to the Canadian border. We have your money and phone. We caught Stuart, David and John. Of course those are not their real names. We arrested Isabel too," said the policeman.

"You arrested her?" asked Giovanna. "Why? But..."

"We will tell you everything after we interview them. Do you have a place to stay?" asked the policeman.

"No, I don't. But maybe I can go to a hotel. Could you please call a hotel? Please tell them I will pay when I get my money and credit card back."

"No," said Elsa, "You can stay at my house. You had a terrible time. My husband Fred and I will look after you."

"Thank you. That's very kind of you," said Giovanna. "But I don't want to be any trouble..."

"You won't be any trouble. I want you to stay," said Elsa.

"We will contact you tomorrow," said the policeman. "Go back to Elsa's house and have a rest."

That night, Giovanna stayed with Elsa and Fred. They lived in a beautiful old house. It was very peaceful. Elsa made stew and bread, and lemon pie. After dinner, Giovanna went to bed and slept for ten hours.

The next morning, when she woke up, the sunlight was coming into her room and the birds outside were singing. She got out of bed and walked to the window.

I'm in the forest! she thought. She opened the window and a gentle breeze came into the room.

She walked downstairs. Elsa and Fred were sitting at the kitchen table.

"Did you sleep well?" asked Elsa.

"Yes, I did. I slept very well," said Giovanna.

"I'll make some fresh coffee and some breakfast. Is egg and toast OK?"

"That sounds great, thank you," she said.

"The policeman called. He will come here at eleven am. It's ten thirty now," said Elsa.

Giovanna was drinking her second cup of coffee when the policeman came to the house.

He sat down and Elsa gave him a cup of coffee.

"So what happened?" asked Giovanna.

"It seems Isabel is not a very good friend," said the policeman. "When you told her about your two million dollars, she decided to steal it from you."

"What? Steal my money?" Giovanna was shocked.

"Isabel and her boyfriend made a plan. They needed help, so they asked two friends to join them.

"The first part of the plan was to invite you to Seattle. You said 'yes' and told Isabel the day and time of your flight from New York. Then, they found an empty house in Roosevelt. It's an area north of the university. The owners are in Europe on vacation. We talked to the owners. They didn't know anything about the plan. They don't know Isabel or the men.

"The second part of their plan was this: Stuart meets you at the airport. He tells you he is Isabel's friend. He tells you Isabel is working and he will take you to Isabel's apartment. But he doesn't take you to her apartment. He takes you to the empty house in Roosevelt. The other men are there. Isabel is there too, but she is not in the house. She is in the garage. He tells you they have Isabel. He says they will kill Isabel if you don't give them all the money in your bank account.

"If you say 'no', they will let you talk to Isabel on the phone. Isabel will cry and scream and say, 'The men are hurting me! Help! Give them the money!' They are sure you will give them the money to save Isabel.

"Then, when they have the money, Isabel and Stuart and the other two men will share the money between them and go to Canada."

Giovanna was quiet. She was very shocked.

"Isabel is a terrible friend!" said Elsa. "I am very pleased the police caught Isabel and the three men."

"So the other two men were John Smith and David Jones," said Giovanna.

"Yes," said the policeman. "Of course Smith and Jones are not their real names."

"But their plan didn't work," said Elsa.

"No," said the policeman. "Giovanna got away from Stuart, so they tried to make a new plan. Stuart went to look for Giovanna, and Isabel waited at the house in Roosevelt with John and David. But Giovanna saw Stuart near Isabel's apartment, rented a car, and followed him to the house in Roosevelt.

"When Giovanna saw Isabel making coffee in the house, Isabel was waiting for Stuart to find Giovanna. But Giovanna found Isabel. Isabel was shocked to see Giovanna. So she said, 'It's dangerous! Go away!' But Giovanna broke the door down, and took Isabel out of the house."

"After that, we drove to a shopping mall, but Stuart found us," said Giovanna.

"Did you give your phone to Isabel?" asked the policeman.

"Yes," said Giovanna. "Isabel said, 'Give me your phone. I'll look at a map.' So I gave her my phone."

"She downloaded a tracking app on it, so her friends could follow you," said the policeman. "They were tracking your location all the time. Then, you went to a convenience store. I guess when you were in the store, Isabel called Stuart. Then Isabel went to the restroom and ran out of the convenience store through the emergency exit door at the back. Stuart was waiting behind the convenience store. He and Isabel drove away.

"Then, David and John came. They said, 'We are detectives.' You believed them, so you got in their car."

"I understand," said Giovanna. "I was very lucky."

"I think so too," said Elsa. "I think those people were very dangerous."

"There is one thing, I don't understand," said Giovanna.

"What's that?" asked the policeman.

"They took my credit card and ID and everything. They had my bank PIN number. But why did the bank give the money to John?"

"The bank didn't give the money to a man," said the policeman. "They gave the money to Isabel. The bank thought they were giving the money to you. You and Isabel look similar. You are the same height. You are the same age. Isabel wore a wig. It was the same colour and style as your hair."

"Oh," said Giovanna.

"Yes," said the policeman. "I think Isabel bought the wig before you came to Seattle. She saw your photos on Facebook. It was part of the plan."

Giovanna was quiet for a few minutes. Then, she said, "I'm shocked. Why did Isabel do this to me? When we were at school we were not very close friends, but she was a nice girl. Well, I thought she was a nice girl."

"I think her boyfriend is the bad one. Isabel is in love with him. Stuart likes money. He wanted a lot of money. Isabel saw a chance to steal your money. But, everything is OK. We took the rental car back to the company, and we have your suitcase, bag, phone and money.

We will take you to the bank now."

"Thank you," said Giovanna.

"What are you going to do?" said Elsa. "Are you going to go back to New York?"

"I think so. I have no friends here, and no place to stay, so…"

"Why don't you stay here for a few days? You can stay with us. We will take you sightseeing. Washington is a beautiful state. We can take you to some wonderful places."

"That's very kind of you," said Giovanna. Are you sure?"

"Of course," said Fred. "Please stay for a few days. We are old and we have no children. We rarely have visitors. We will enjoy it if you stay for a few days."

Giovanna smiled. "OK. Thank you. I'd love to stay."

THANK YOU

Thank you for reading Danger in Seattle. (Word count: 6,442) We hope you enjoyed it. The next book in the City Thriller series is Adventure in Rome.

There are quizzes about this book on our free study site I Talk You Talk Press EXTRA. http://italk-youtalk.com

If you would like to read more graded readers, please visit our website http://www.italkyoutalk.com

Other Level 2 graded readers include
Adventure in Rome
Andre's Dream
A Passion for Music
Christmas Tales
Don't Come Back
Finders Keepers…
Marcy's Bakery
Men's Konkatsu Tales
Salaryman Secrets!
Stories for Halloween
The Perfect Wedding
The House in the Forest

The School on Bolt Street
Train Travel
Trouble in Paris
Women's Konkatsu Tales

ABOUT THE AUTHOR

I Talk You Talk Press is a Japan-based publisher of language textbooks, graded readers and language learning/teaching resources.

Our team is made up of highly experienced language teachers and translators, who have all studied at least one additional language to an advanced level.

This experience enables us to design our materials from the perspective of both the teacher and the learner. We consult with both teachers and language learners when designing our textbooks and graded readers, and test our materials extensively in the classroom before publication.

We are a fast-growing press, and currently publish graded readers for learners of English. We publish new graded readers monthly.

www.ingramcontent.com/pod-product-compliance
Lightning Source LLC
Chambersburg PA
CBHW022350040426
42449CB00006B/812